With a Stranger's Eyes

Also by Jeremy Hooker

Jeremy Hooker

With a Stranger's Eyes

Shearsman Books

First published in the United Kingdom in 2025 by
Shearsman Books Ltd
PO Box 4239
Swindon
SN3 9FN

Shearsman Books Ltd Registered Office
30–31 St. James Place, Mangotsfield, Bristol BS16 9JB
(this address not for correspondence)

EU AUTHORISED REPRESENTATIVE:
Lightning Source France
1 Av. Johannes Gutenberg, 78310 Maurepas, France
Email: compliance@lightningsource.fr

www.shearsman.com

ISBN 978-1-84861-970-8

ACKNOWLEDGEMENTS

Some poems in this book appeared first in the following
publications, whose editors I wish to thank:

*Agenda, Planet, Poetry Wales, Poetry Salzburg Review, Red Poets,
Scintilla, Temenos Academy Review, The Brazen Head* (Australia).

I also wish to thank Christopher Meredith for close readings
that helped me to improve some poems in this book.

Contents

3. THE ROWAN TREE

1. DUTCH GIRL

Dutch Girl

Dearest, how
can you be 'late'
when your very absence
is my companion?

You are here
                    you are there
a woman by herself
musing in a room.
Is that my letter in your hand?

Alone, with maps on the wall,
you are a world.

2

So close, so far
you bring your country
to me – the brick streets,
cycle paths and Saxon villages,
windmills & dykes,
a heron flying over
or stick-still among the reeds.

I recall such pleasure
with you, my love.

Clay & water & fire
were our elements,

all our senses alive
and most of all, touch.

3

I think of the Waddenzee
and Schiermonnikoog
of the ash-grey monks –
sand island with cemeteries
of men thrown up by the sea
and known only to God.

I see fields of blue clay,
pasture that was sea
at the land's edge,
cattle and gulls
on salt grass at the marge.
It is all you, and not you.
There is more to see, always –
the rooms, the streets,
the tangible, elusive now,
not fading, only too far to reach.

4

Martini Tour, 'the old grey one',
towered over us on days
at the Grote Markt, where,
in the crush of pedals, knees and feet
we would walk gingerly

around the stalls, where
men sliced cheese for us
to taste, and we bought
vegetables, fish, and fruit.
You would then load me
with shopping bags, string
biting into my fingers,
and we would walk home
laughing at my burden,
complete with happiness.

5

Winter brought skaters to ponds
in the Noorderplantsoen
old and young together,
whole families – parents,
grandparents, children,
circling, falling, helping
each other up, red-faced
with exertion, bright-eyed,
shouting and laughing.

Once an ice-storm silenced the city.
Birch trees bent like hoops
under the weight of ice. Pylons
like steel giants buckled at the knees.
When I opened the door
my beard instantly froze.

Memory brings bitter cold,
a painting by Averkamp
ringing with silence.
But we were at the window,
together in the warm,
relishing sublime emptiness
of silent streets, cars immobilised,
gables tusked with ice.

6

Often I return
to the Korreweg, not
the house only, on the corner
of Balistraat, but the life
to which you welcomed me.

I remember the garden
we climbed to, squirming
through a trap door
onto the roof – like being
born again in middle age.

And on the roof
                    sunflowers
and you bending over them
face to face, my lady
of the sunflowers.

Around us, spires,
clocktowers, smoke

from a factory,
houseboats and barges
on the canal,
a heron flying over –
      Groningen,
the city I came to love.

7

Time paints me pictures,
landscapes and portraits,
meadows with cows and horses,
riotous families, contemplative
women, and faces, always faces,
often the same face, young and old.

Grave and wondering,
self-seeing, the artists of your land
look out of time, beyond
comings and goings
of generations, past loss and grief.
A time that is forever shines in their eyes.

Is that what memory can be?
Can our time live,
or must it be buried with the years?
I know the life we made
will be with me until I die.

Love isn't like a body
buried or given to the flames

but part of our very being
with a life after life
that, alas, we cannot touch.

She brings flowers into my home

for Elin

1

She did not love me at first,
a stranger who appeared
in the middle of the night,
and woke up to a foreign land
with cycle paths and windmills,
flat pastures and fields of blue clay
taken from the sea, which
always pressed at the land's edge,
promising to return.

And the people were strange to me.
They look one in the face
with a directness that shows
no use for English irony
as if to say: 'And who are you?'

2

Who was I then?
A youngish man with a broken life
who was being loved back whole.

How should she care about that,
seeing an intruder in her home,
a stranger with whom she was required
to sit at table, disliking the way

he opened his mouth
and chewed his food, regarding me
with a critical eye that I was unaware of,
as I floated in the warmth of her mother's love?

3

Now, though, she crosses the North Sea
to visit me in Wales, and buys me
daffodils – no longer a girl,
but a woman in middle years
with two boys and a grown-up son.

And she is fighting the addiction
that ruined her mother's life,
and fighting it successfully
with willpower and therapy.

'No', we say, 'life isn't easy',
as we look into the past, seeing
the woman we both loved so much,
who would have given her life for us,
if she hadn't been taken by alcohol.
What sadness we have known, what grief,
and how we have shared it.
Yet still, she says, 'There is only love.'

2. LIVING IN WALES

Aberystwyth

Starlings at dusk seemed
to put on a display especially
for visitors over the wrecked pier.
Herring gulls shrilled on chimneys
or menaced sun-worshippers
eating ice-cream or chips.
Huk huk, they cried, behaving
as if they owned the town.

In storm, seas crashed
over the promenade, and flung pebbles
at boarded-up house fronts, behind which
heavy furniture inched across the floor.
A rag of red weed
clung to a top story back window.

On halcyon days, it was paradise
and the sea at evening
would be streaked with arrows of gold.

For me, it was the town of lost love.
On certain days, mountain peaks
would appear across the bay
as if they were volcanic islands
in the tropics – heavenly, like a future
one may dream of but will not live to enjoy.

A Stranger in Wales

remembering Carol Ann

1

You left me with a dream.

On the narrow lane
above the Teifi, where
it drops, foaming, to Cenarth
and the coracle fishers and the Falls
rose-bay willowherb
was filling the autumn air
with a smoke of seeds.
Swallows were gathering above.
Preseli showed a blue dome to the west.

2

*Our fingers touch; we feel them
Ache to hold, saying goodbye...*
words of a poem I started
but could not finish,
lines which, after sixty years,

                   still sing in my head.

3

The language on your lips
was an invitation
to a poetry that was beyond me.

It spoke of Yr Wyddfa
and Enlli, island of saints.
                    In your voice
enchantment
shone on the simplest things
which made for me a new world
in the oldest places.

4

Poets a thousand years ago
sang the land
you introduced me to.
Bards of lost wars, magicians,
and the boy poet who never died.
All sang the land, and as if emerging
from hedgerow flowers, beautiful women
appeared
                    Branwen Olwen Blodeuwedd

5

But what suffering goes to the making of a people.
Cymry defeated, Cymry colonized.

You left me no illusion.
                    Beyond romance
there was a new poetry:
a hard imagination,
converting old metres to new means,

alive to work in factory and foundry
and to life under pitwheels
in terraced valleys, quickened
by the agony of defeat.

6

It was a black winter when you left.
Y Felin Penpompren,
the old mill we should have shared,
was desolate and cold.
At night, listening
to every sound for a footstep,
I felt, in a leaf scratching at the door,
or wind rattling the latch
                                    a lurch of hope.

Years later in another life,
I would suddenly look up
from working in the garden
and sense you coming down the lane
towards me, visible for an instant,
but vanishing.
                        And it was always
the final leaving,
smoke of seeds on the air,
swallows gathering, and you
in your absence becoming
spirit of the whole land
where I was a stranger.

Return to Llangwyryfon

for Sue
and for Joe and Emily

1
In early March, curlews
would return to their breeding ground
in marshy ground above the house
and cuckoos called and called
all day from late April into June.
In winter, fieldfares flocked to berries
in the hedges and a rare red kite
came down from the mynydd.
At times, it seemed
the parish belonged to the birds.

But this was farming country,
with farmers and shepherds –
our neighbours –
tending cattle and flocks of sheep.

Unpacking, we were welcomed
by Glyn Davies and his step-son,
Dilwyn, a big lad with a voice
that could be heard shouting
to his sheepdog in the next parish.
In the year of drought, he brought us
water in a shining milk churn.
Old Mr Morris, wearing a sack
over his shoulders, leaned
over the fence of his field and greeted us.

2

It felt like a hidden place,
disconnected from the world
but there were views
of distant mountains – Pumlumon
and Cadair Idris, and Yr Wyddfa.
a small white peak far to the north:
steppping stones through the Welsh heartland.

Best of all I loved Mynydd Bach,
where the sun rose for us
unless it was hidden in mist.
With its cairns and remains
of lead mines and ruins of houses
built in a night, it smelled
of sheep droppings and grass in the sun,
and rose above Lon Sais,
the lane which translated
as Englishman's Road, because
a gentleman had tried to build
his house on common land
and saw it knocked down by men
dressed as women, who knew
where they belonged and he did not

3

When dew was on the grass
I would walk out with a child on my back
who would sing out when spotting a mushroom
which we would take home and eat for breakfast.

I would make up stories from local features
to entertain them – like the Avanc
that lived in the cold waters of Llyn Eiddwen.

Passing the house one winter morning
I looked in and saw you kneeling
on the hearth to light the fire.
Our eyes met
and I thought: *it will be*
 all right between us for ever.
I call it thought, but somehow
it rose from deep within
or came from far off
as if it were simply there
and my mind had no part in it.

4

One glorious morning, walking
up the lane past the waterfall,
I looked back and was amazed
to see the house where we lived
transformed to a cube of light.

Did we really live there then?
This Wales was indeed a visionary country.
But it wasn't ours.
I could not claim that we belonged.
Everywhere objects spoke a different language
and everything we saw and touched
existed in other words, old

but ever-present, with a history
that had entered deep into the being of things –
streams and tree trunks and leaves,
fields and the soil under our feet
and although we could not see them
there were people long-dead, who,
like Glyn and Dilwin and Mr Morris,
came between us and the sun and the dark
calling the cattle in and rounding up the sheep.

Welsh Cloud

Nimbostratus
might be designated
the national cloud
that brings a special rain.
But there are mackerel skies
all over fish scales,
 and cirrus, and lovely
cumulus, white
as the washing that can now
be hung out in gardens
where, forty years ago,
even the daisies were black.

They are worth a song,
even the thuderclouds,
anvils on which a mighty blacksmith
could shoe the horse
of Bendigeidfran fab Llyr.
But, best of all, the bright-edged
or those with openings,
ruined castles, or clouds
that resemble giant puffballs
and allow blue sky, and sun
to which the yellows of spring,
daffodil and dandelion,
primrose and celandine,
reach up and open their faces.

Standing Stone

What is it but tongue of a language
we do not know?
Yet, coming upon one unexpectedly
in some field, a stark object
that declares the work of hands
like our own, and worship
of a Spirit that seems to call us back
we shiver with anticipation – but of what?

Against the palms of our hands
it is sheer stone, like a door
we cannot push open.
What souls has it witnessed
in their making, who have passed
into earth's cradle, from which
they were born – earth
that is always only earth?

Erect, as if a boast of man's glory
what the stone shows us
is the fragment we stand on.

It has survived the ages.
But nothing, it seems, could be more dead.
Yet when we look away, we dream
that it too dreams, throwing off
the shrouded stillness
and calling up a company
long since fallen
that dances, dances, in a ring

all are part of,
while the stone catches
the light of the moon
and glows with the fires of the sun.

Stonemason, sculptor, mariner

for Philip Chatfield

A man who came alive from a wreck
off the Cornish coast, in which
friends died, who clung
to a barnacled rock, sea-washed,
jagged for a hand-hold,
which saved his life.

 What stone gave him
he gives back
with imaginative touch
shaping images lovingly
with chisel and hammer:
the Virgin of Tintern Abbey,
the Madonna of Capel-y-ffin –
mothering figures
that gather the silence about them
and turn the master's work to praise.

Jesse Figure

(St Mary's Priory Church, Abergavenny)
for Bernard Harrington

Was this the ancestor of Jesus?

This broken thing, lying
under the new stained glass
in an atmosphere of polish and piety,
organ music rising religiously
high up to the roof,
lying like something cast up,
figurehead from a wreck
out of place on the tiled floor,
like a rude noise in a space
set apart for prayer and meditation.

With time, Jesse has become
more like the tree he was hewn from,
an old god of the oakwoods,
a majestic, blood-letting titan,
all power of execution gone with the Tree
whose root he was, yet still
with a kind of power
informing this ruined hulk.

Who, then, were Jesse's progeny?
Certainly, this mighty figure
could have brought a sword,
and wielded it,
some great two-handed shatterer
of skulls and trimmer of torsos.

I can imagine him fathering the Marcher lords,
and leading them like a giant
up to his thighs in Welsh blood –
master of these men
that lie close by, wooden or alabaster
figures, with hands crossed
on armoured chests, one with a monk
kneeling at his feet, a Beadsman
praying for his soul, eternally.

Arranged thus, these lords
with their ladies resemble Jesse's progeny,
masterful men brought in from the land
they conquered, this border
where now hedges are white with may
under the Black Mountains, and slowly
their preserved castles fall
to the weather stone by stone.

Is this how the story ends?
Wooden man, I do not come to mock.
If I could, I would see you as a Lear
in his brokenness, an old man
dead to the power that has brought him
to this end, weak, indeed,
but with the finality of love.

In Brecon Cathedral

1. The Font

1.

What were they thinking of.
the Norman carvers
who placed this monster
with a clear view up the aisle
of the dark figure hanging over the altar?

They were amused, perhaps, lightening
the task with grim humour
as they hewed a savage face from the stone.
But why did they add birds and animals
and a scorpion, and all twisted –
a hellish company – which was,
I suppose the point.

2

They could not know
this would be a soldier's church
commemorating brave men
from many wars –
Welsh archers from Agincourt
and soldiers of the World Wars,
South Wales Borderers,
men remembered by flags
and plaques and dedicated pews.

3

Think of the babies baptised
in the mouth of this monster,
immersed, as it were, in the jaws
of the Green Man.
How they would have howled
at this introduction to a wet, cold world.
Yet here they were held lovingly
in the monster's brutish grip.
But their parents were not deceived,
and although they could not imagine
Gallipoli and Agincourt, they knew
the Scorpion's sting and the fate
that awaits the dead, beyond this world.

2. The Cresset Stone

What is this life
but stumbling in the dark?

As monks knew making their way
precariously to Vigil.

So they lit candles at the Cresset Stone
and carried them in trembling hands.

Waxen light guided them
over cracks in the floor.

Things they knew by heart
made them shake in the cold.

Only light could save them from a fall –
only candle light, but an image

of the light they prayed for,
that they hoped one blessed day

to be immersed in, embraced,
and know in love, but never see.

3. On the Painting called *Peace*
for Liam Guilar

Heartfelt, but if we fail
to be convinced, we may think
Isaiah wouldn't have deemed it
worth a sparrow's fart.

But the artist's soul was in it.
It wasn't his fault
that he was a Victorian.

Isaiah wasn't of that kind.
But suppose he had taken up a brush
to render his dream of peace.

We can only guess,
but, surely, the lion
would have been a real beast

and ready, on a day
without vision
to maul and devour the child.

At the Grave of Raymond Williams

In the church of Clydog
alongside the graveyard
where he lies, with Joy, his wife
beside him, another man's wife
has a tomb inscribed 'native of this place'.

As he was, man of 'Border Country'
and the Black Mountains. And to us
everywhere, a man
who made hope possible
instead of despair.
     Such confidence
from this railway man's son,
scholarship boy and tank commander
who fought panzers in the Ardennes
and returned to Cambridge
where he was never at home.

A modest man, he taught us
with keywords that redefined
where we stand, and reformed
ideas of culture and society.

'What breaks capitalism,' he said,
'is capitalists.'
     Such optimistic words!
But how far Pandy is from Westminster,
which might be on a planet
in another galaxy, though
its decrees reach to the roots

of life in the Marches
and everywhere in our benighted isles.

I felt what he felt when he dug
a trench or put his hands
into the soil, and the life
of the dead reached back to him.
But his was a materialism
I could not believe in, finally.

Yet there was matter
in everything he said and did,
and this place, which was
his 'only landscape', bleeds
for want of his wisdom and his love.

What I feel as I stand by his grave
is an abrupt end and a deep emptiness,
a void where a mind stopped,
with words unspoken in which
we could have found hope.
            Here, too, a heart
came to rest in native earth.

The Burning Tree

In memory of Anne Cluysenaar

Thank God, Anne,
your terrible death is behind you.
We may think of you now, free
as you were on your smallholding,
looking for mushrooms in the meadow,
riding your cob into Wentwood Forest.

Most companionable poet,
you sought to speak with others
across the centuries – Henry Vaughan
in your Usk Valley, Alfred Russell Wallace
and the scribe of Gilgamesh.

What are thousands of years
to poets who contemplate death?
Words are part of the landscape
that embraces the living and the dead.
Language, you knew,
follows the rivers and the hills,
and grows with the trees.
Most of all, poetry is language
that shapes the world
in which we can breathe:
a Tree of Life that is
half in leaf and half in flame,
green and burning, but never consumed.

Gwenallt

after M. Wynn Thomas

1

Ferocious old man:
what could I,
fresh from England,
make of such a face?

Drawn tight on the skull,
it was like damaged parchment
written in a language unknown to me –
script of the poetry
of an archaic culture.
What could it be but dead?

2

I might have spoken to him.
But what could I have said
as we passed in corridors
of the old college facing the sea?
There was a language between us
that was a broken bridge.

3

Knowledge of his life
brought him closer, into the modern world,
this man on fire
who had known both
a bardic chair and a prison cell,
whose father's death in a fall of molten metal
in the steelworks
                        burned into his soul.
He was a pilgrim from a dream
 of human perfection to Calvary
and the sin that blasted Eden,
 and in and behind all
he saw the figure of Christ.
                        He was Jeremiah
who flayed his people whoring after false gods.
As for humankind, what were we
but wolves howling for the blood of salvation?

4

Reading *Rhydcymerau*
in translation, his words seared me
with their anguish and fury and love.
I could say he mourned the loss
of his home and native culture,
but it wasn't loss; it was destruction
that tore out the heart of his land
with the claws of the English beast.

5

In place of healing trees
on land of Tir-bach and Esgeir-ceir
conifer shadows darken ruins
where a family once gathered,
and moss brings a sort of comfort
to stone of fallen walls.

But I will not insult the man
with elegy, or lessen his ferocity
with emollient words.
                        Let me see him
   as the Jeremiah he was,

                              prophet
   of the death we have dealt a nation,
   and the doom we are bringing on our own.

Carreg Waldo

'Pa Beth yw bod yn gwladgarwch? Cadw ty
Mewn cwmwl tystion'?

for M. Wynn Thomas

1

It looks lonely here –
one stone
bearing a man's name:
    polished bluestone,
        brother to the stones
they say Merlin spirited to Stonehenge.

Some say that this man was a myth.
        Say, rather,
that he was a poet, and a man of peace.

2

This is Waldo's bro,
        his country
peopled with friends and neighbours,
a singular man, who laboured in the fields
in kinship with men and women
united by a language and a faith.

      You could say
that in this land of stone
there isn't a stone that doesn't tell a story,

of fire or rot or ages of rain,
of sedimentation
                    and metamorphosis.
You may see it as a world of change,
and the dumb eloquence of rock.

3

How will time stand
where everything is in process
forming and dissolving?
How will the brute earth speak
unless with the poet's word?

            And what of the clouds, what are they
but native as the rock, and the monoliths
that were the work of men and women
who worshiped the life of the earth,
and the moon and the sun and the stars,
                        and gave human meaning
to what seems barren under the naked sky?

4

Day touches Preseli with wands of light.
It is all now, and ageless, and millions of years,
a land magicked ito being,
            a place of healing
                            spoken and loved.

And what are the clouds, the shadow-bearers
obscuring and revealing, and passing
eternally passing
                    over the lonely stone?

Note: the epigraph is from Waldo Williams: 'What is love
of country? Keeping house / Among a cloud of witnesses',
translated by Tony Conran.

David Jones at Capel-y-ffin

for Peter Wakelin

1

It is a delicate art he learns –
   whiteness
of the paper showing through
as the pencil moves gently
in his fingers.
           And, yes, it is true,
the universal is revealed
through the particular thing.

2

He is a man entranced
by the hills' rhythms
and the bright counter-rhythms
of Honddu and Nant Bwch
as they stream in the sun.

3

What do the trees mean
that form circles
which might be sacred enclosures
or hint at an image
of the blighted, holy wood
of blood and sap?

4

If it can ever be a new world
it is here, it is now, in this place
for a man in love,
as darkness seems to vanish
at a boundary that does not separate
flesh and spirit, but joins them –
a marchland
of hills and streams, and ponies
that might have survived ancient battles
grazing flank to flank
on grassy, trenched earth.

5

It is all real enough, and all a symbol
like the woman he loves – Petra, who is
Blodeuwedd, Flora, Mary.

This is the moment, as near
to perfection as human life comes.

And, of course, it cannot last
as his fingers move delicately
on the paper, discovering
new vision
in this country of the March.

Seeking Idris Davies

On a showery evening
in April, hills leaden in the wet,
travelling from Rhymney
to Fochriw and Bedlinog across the moor,
I think of Idris Davies and his poems.

It is a miserable scene
which must have been worse
during his short life
when the agony of the pit
coincided with the wasteland
of Strike and Slump and Depression.
But who can describe a life
of such courage and passion?
And who can measure the ecstasy
of a poet lying in sunshine on the green hills
reading Shelley and listening to the larks?
Think, too, of the blade of anger
eviscerating the plunderers of his people.

'A poet of his time and place'?
How shall we find him
now the pitwheels have ceased to turn
and the hills are restored
to horses and sheep?
How shall we know him
except by a music in the heart
and bells ringing, all the bells
ringing, across Glamorgan and Gwent?

In Memory of Norman Schwenk

for Deborah Kay Davies

An American in Cardiff
you were always a man from Nebraska –
though a follower of Glamorgan cricket,
which in recent years
has been a hopeless pursuit.

A loving man, you naturally espoused
'the pleasure which there is in life itself.'
Good companion, teacher
who nourished the art of your students,
you were a poet
who did not despise a limerick,
humorous verse, affectionate,
with wit at the expense of pretentious fools.

Norman,
who will sit with me now,
two old men at Caesar's
or in the Chinese restaurant
at Riverside, gossiping and happy
to be together and with our beloved wives,
though straining to hear what the other says?

Quakers Yard

for Philip and Zélie Gross

George Fox preached here
and George Borrow visited
searching for Quakers.
What he found were only the dead
in their burial ground - an elbow
of land between two rivers.

The place was known as Rhyd y Grug,
Ford of the Rustling Water.
The sound and the silence
never die. Even the traffic
over the bridge seems to pass
with a muted sound, as
you stand by the graves
imagining an inner light
that spreads into the light of day
touching leaves trembling on the alders
and glinting on the rustling waters.

Haunted House

Children called it
the haunted house.
It may have been because
an angry man lived here.
              In what was then
that most communal place
no neighbour would turn out
to bear his coffin.
              Or perhaps
it was the surroundings:
Black Brook, and the jagged face
of the overgrown quarry
where rock had been hewn
to fortify Deep Navigation mine.

              And always, here,
that sense of underground workings
that leak into sunlight
with a feeling of watery dark.

Whatever it was, I do not know
why children passed this house
with a tremor of fear.
What I do know are days and nights
when I would have given my life
to feel the touch of a ghostly hand.

On Gelligaer Common

1

A wild horse with its hoof trapped
in the rusted springs of a mattress.
Do we deserve to survive?

2

Look around. In clear weather
the views are sublime:
Brecon Beacons and Black Mountains
far to the north.
South, a sliver of Severn Sea
and the Somerset coast.

Underfoot, a trace of Roman road.
But the land embraces more:
remains of ancient settlements,
site of a chapel dedicated to a Dark Age martyr.
A stone slant against the sky
commemorates an Irish warrior.
Picts, too, marauded here.
There's even a tale of Arthur
attached to the heathery spurs.

Horses, said to be descendants
of pit ponies, run wild
on grown-over slagheaps.

3

So much in this space,
where our leavings
speak of us ambiguously,
whether shepherds or pitmen,
or the man from Sussex,
asleep in his car, who will wake up
to search for magic mushrooms.

4

What can we say of our kind?
Was beauty always kin to horror?

The dumb, pittted earth
we have tended and despoiled
shows what we call a face
as if it too were human.

The wounded horse strains to free itself,
but the rusted springs hold.

Cuckoos at Deri

for Debbie and and Ian Tog Jenkins

No cuckoo
again –
       a deadness
at the heart of sound
through May & June.

No cuckoo
but news of cuckoos
in our friends' garden,
two of them
muscling eggs
out of a blackbird's nest
to bring the summer in.

On the Road to Senghenydd

As you approach,
it might be anywhere in Wales –
moorland, with reeds
that scratch the sight,
a huddle of sheep in the lee
of dry-stone walls – handiwork
of the centuries - light
that reveals distant mountains
or cloud that shows only cloud.
And, indeed, what is there to see?

And then the hill road
that twists, precipitous,
turning on itself, descending
as if out of daylight
into the dark of the earth.
Here a gorse bush blazes,
a ruined building, and the village
where, once, on a sunny day
in October, the world ended.

Do not imagine you can imagine it.
Do not suppose you know
what grief is, or terror, or courage
of men entering an inferno
to rescue their kind. Today
you may think the scene medieval,
like a picture of hell.
But you will know nothing
unless you catch a distant echo

from the very ground, where
a father calls for his son,
and a son cries for his father.

Passing through Aberfan

Conifers on the ridge,
where the black river
poured down, reveal nothing.
It is the house fronts
that seem to speak – blank faces
that suggest what may lie within:
children getting ready
for another day in school,
thinking of friends, or of work
done or neglected, imagining
what freedom may be like.
Years on, for parents, it will be
for ever the same day,
buried in time, futureless.

Shadowland

In memory of Jim Davies

1

A calm pool where the mine was,
a place re-created for leisure,
and beside it, a light on a post,
where a cormorant hunches, brooding.
But what light is there
for this valley condemned to deadness?

So much has ended here.
It seems the very clouds erupt
from the closed pits, bringing
a pall of blackness, a memory
of wild flowers, faces dirty with soot.

Yet this was where a world was made,
where power drove wheels and keels
of an empire, and dis-empowered
the makers who constructed it.

2

Spare a song for the men and their wives,
for children and grandchildren
who ask why they are here,
who stumble, who grope for a purpose.

3

Resistance was the word:
communities, societies, culture,
chapels that are now show rooms:
realm of 'the miner's next step' –
which was into the grave.
But here was a dream held close to the heart –
a dream of justice for all, a dream
of making a life
fit for men and women and their families.

An iron word killed it,
a word policed and pitiless.
Now the land is green again,
all the grime gone, all the grind.

4

We may visit in a dream
a world below the world,
and wander, lost, or crouch
anticipating the fire of nightmare.

Comes a blue sky with such clarity.
Comes the mercy of rain,
falling on gritty paths and black brooks
which a dry season had turned to torrents of stone.

5

Resistance was the poets' word –
spoken, and sung, and whispered.
It was what the people gave,
and not only with the tongue.
Think rather of song
with the whole body behind it,
yearning and passionate,
and not one person's alone,
whether sung by one or by many.
Think of betrayal, dust choking the throat,
of abandonment, of an iron language
that deals death to a people.

6

It is beautiful here, with the land
restored to greenness, a buzzard
over the valley, a heron following the river,
where salmon swim again.
Daisies are white once more
and sheets can be hung outdoors.
The Deep Navigation
once took men down from sunlight
to workface, under the land
we now look at, walking or standing
with empty hands, watching clouds
and the moving shadows of cloud.

How they flow, opening on light,
closing on darkness. But do not call this
Death's country only. Remember
the laughter, the pub talk,
the voice of pulpit and platform.
                    Recall above all
love whispering on the hills and in the valley,
and passion of miners' lodges
that would reshape the world.
                    Remember
the fate of hope, broken on an iron word.

Bless Treharris Park

Bless the Tulip Tree,
the exotic one, lavish
with pink blossom – a festival
come and gone in days.

Bless also the wildings –
starveling snowdrop
and violets, always to be found
in their own place.

Bless the nuthatches
and the squirrels,
the dog and the dog-walker,
and the robin that shows no fear.
Despise no common creature.

Hallow the trench mortar
perched on a boulder
which remembers the men
who marched from here
and did not come back.

Recall with gratitude
the children running wild
in the woods, and inscribing
on war memorial and bridge
their names and loves.

Remember lovingly
the generations of miners
and their families, who
sang and played
at the bandstand, long –
abandoned and open to the sky.

Bless the music, long
since faded into silence
in this place, where a poet,
a redundant miner,
might dream of finding
his voice again, and raising it
in fellowship
to a live community
thronging their beloved park.

3. THE ROWAN TREE

Dialysis: reading Ibn 'Arabi

From the hospital window
high above Cardiff, mist unveils
a glimpse of the Severn.

We lie on our beds, each
attached to a machine.
The book is heavy in my left hand.

Below, a tide from mid-Atlantic
powers inland, past Bristol
towards Gloucester.
I think of water racing,
                              running over sand,
 rolling upriver, and the joy
of surfers and canoeists
                              riding the waves.

I turn a page and read:
                              Love is my creed.
Wherever love's caravan
turns along the way,
that is my belief.

Briefly, an image
of holiday traffic on the M4
passes through my mind.

A gull flies past, on the tide of air.

Everything, I read, *speaks of*
                    a reality beyond.

Nurses circle among the beds,
bringing kindness
or a quip to make us smile.

Each patient is alive
to the present moment
or asleep, or adrift
between memory and dream.

I take up my notebook
and scrawl 'love's caravan' –
which calls up a trek with camels
through a wilderness of sand.

As my blood runs,
I settle with the Sufi
who tells me present things
occlude the divine life
that throbs in every part of the universe.

Through veils of light and dark
day brings to the window
 glimpses of river and bridge,
a flash of water, and, just visible
as a dim shape, the far shore.

The Rowan Tree

1

Slender tree
which I have watched
winter-naked
and in bud and blossom
and falling leaves,
tree that stands alone
which I have observed
from the window, admiring
such resilience
and simple beauty
of graceful silvery-grey
branches moving
with the winds during
these seasons of grief.

I have loved many trees
since I was a boy:
old gnarly oaks
and smooth-bole beeches,
silvery birch, elms
that fell to ruin in the hedge,
sycamore and chestnuts
of candle and prickly fruit,
alders, with which I stood
by many streams, even
the fir that brings darkness
to every season.

In a life so enriched
I have recognized
many trees, and understood
secrets of the forest,
ancient lore and worship
of The Tree of Life.
I have heard the voice
of the dreaming Rood.
But for me, this stripling
by the front door,
this is the one I choose
to be my sacred tree.

2

Poetry is praise, as
from ancient times
Welsh poets have known.
First, though, and last
it is making, and now,
with ruins of language,
words without substance,
shucked of meaning,
spiritless – with these
in the air we breathe,
a poet has to work
to make a living thing.

The time is dark
in which I write,
with people confined

to their homes, and afraid,
like memories of an age
of pestilence. Less severe
for me than for many,
since I am housebound,
unable to breathe
the common air, and near
the end of my days, able to walk
only as far as the little tree.

3

Mountain ash
it is called, familiar
in this area, once green
that is now green
again, burying the mines
and coal-measures
and all the history
that killed, but also made lives
and animated communities –
abandoned to forces
that scar the earth, and move on.

What is power,
the powerless ask, looking
at their scarred hands?

Here, the Giant's Bite
looks down on the valley –
quarried for stone,

from which viaduct,
bridges and houses
were built laboriously.

Other giants have stalked
and stalk this land:
Disease, Squalor, Want.
Richard Trevithick,
the Cornish giant, built
his railway, and initiated
an industry that circled
the globe with iron rails.
But what is power when
the body fails, and a people
is left powerless?

4

Little tree
(if I may) I love you.
Fortunately,
you do not love me.
How tragic it would be
if you did. If there
were nothing in the world
that is not human.
Already we have left
our mark all over
the body of Earth
in glacier and desert
and in the deepest sea.

All praise for you, tree,
who know nothing of me.

Reach down, slender rowan,
as you lift limbs to the sun.
Let me imagine you
piercing the soil, pushing
through grit and coal seam,
rooting through passages
where miners once lay
on their sides, prizing
from brute matter wealth
that helped to build a world
and made others rich.

5

Tree of the coalfield
with white blossom
and scarlet berries
in season, lovers' tree,
and tree to delight the man
risen to daylight
from crawling in dust.
Now you, like we humans
are at risk from disease.
Like us, you face extinction.

Who will protect you now,
Tree of protection?
What spirit of the goddess?

Where will you fly
with your eagle-feather leaves?
Guardian tree, set in place
to ward off spirits of the dead,
who will save you now?
When the evil eye is upon you,
how will you keep evil from the land?

Names speak your virtues:
Quickberry
   Quickbeam
      Quicken Tree
      Quicken Wood
Saxons knew you as cwicbeam.
Sacred to Thor,
the Norse saw in you
a magic charm. They said
the first woman
was made from your wood.

Quick, companion tree,
I have watched you
through a window
during seasons of grief
and failing health.
It pleases me
that you are no thing
of words, but indifferent
to all I say or think.
A tree simply being,
whatever 'simple' or 'being' mean.

I know, I indulge myself.
All my song, all my address
is illusion. Whatever I ask
there will be no answer,
no other voice but my own
sounding in silence.
And what is prayer?
Is there no voice
but a human voice in all
the intelligible universe?

Winter tree, where, after rain
a rare sun kindles water drops
until, on short, sad days
they break into flame.
Naked tree, which reveals
the village below, in which
George Fox preached
the inner light, and Quakers
lie in their burial ground,
I, who first found love
in another country, feel
strangely content here
among the Glamorgan hills
to make my final home.

6

Rowan tree
that enchants my days
be to me, if only

in imagination,
an old man's staff.
Let me stand with you
against Atlantic gales.
Allow me to warm myself
with your leaves' red glow
against the coming cold.

Man at a window: *six observations*

1

Across the valley,
the mountain,
        Mynydd Eglwysilan
radio masts, a church
dedicated to a saint
who may not have existed.

Buried in the churchyard
after pit disasters,
miners who lived nearby.

2

A buzzard
with its cat's call
turns rising in circles.

Human vision
delights, ascending.

Looking up, the mouse
trembles, eyes
suddenly struck blind.

3

Happiness springs
unintended

with the first crocus
on a February morning.

One bright flower
piercing frozen soil
one flame in the dark.

4

A day without wind
that seems spiritless
yet leaves are dancing
on the mountain ash
where the yellow beak
of a blackbird pecks red fruit.

For the watcher
too, this is a feast.

5

Gull, gull,
lover of sea
and rubbish dump
devotee of plough

take me with you,
the observer asks,
                    let me share
a world that is alive,
where sea roughens
with flying spume
under the west wind.

6

One bright star,
solitary, it seems,
in the whole night sky.

A man alone, with nothing
but the star, whose name
he does not know, to focus on.

How he feels his ignorance
that fills the universe;
and would despair, but

thinks of the young poet
who never died, but lives
steadfast,
for the holiness that is love.

Reflections on Two Welsh Words

I have lived in Wales twice. From 1965 to 1980, I lived, at first alone, in Aberystwyth, and from 1969, with Sue and then our children, at Llangwyryfon in rural Ceredigion. Since 2001, I have lived in south Wales, in the Taff–Bargoed valley, near the site of the Deep Navigation coal mine in what was formerly Glamorgan. I regret that, in spite of several attempts, I have failed to learn Welsh. In consequence the Welsh language has remained for me a haunting 'other'.

The two Welsh words that have bcome especially significant for me are *bro* and *cynefin*. *Bro* may be understood to mean a person's special locality and is often associated with poets, as in Waldo Williams' *bro* in the Preseli mountains. By this definition, my original *bro* would be an area of Hampshire.

Mari Llwyd, my children's teacher in the Welsh school in Llangwyryfon, once kindly described that area, which I had written about in poems in *Englishman's Road*, as my *bro*. It was an honour I was unable to accept. During that period of living in Wales, I could never feel that, compared to a Welsh-language poet, I could claim to be 'of the place'. What this displacement made me more aware of was where I had come from, home ground to which I still felt I belonged.

Cynefin may be understood in English with the wider meaning of homeland or heartland. It implies rootedness in a region or country in all senses: physical, cultural, and spiritual. It involves a sense of belonging. I could never claim to belong in Wales. Living here initially intensified my sense of belonging to my original home ground in the south of England. Later, especially during my second period in Wales, I have come to feel a radical sense of strangeness. This has personal implications: I am a stranger in the area in which I live, and a stranger to the tragic history of the area. Being a stranger has affected my idea of myself as a poet. In tune with the thinking of modernists such as T.S. Eliot, David Jones, and George Oppen, I conceive of the poem as a made object, a thing that stands apart from the poet, an act in a transpersonal 'conversation'. I differ in emphasising its nature as an emotional process. I have finally come to recognize that I am primarily a lyric poet and a love poet.

In between the periods of living in Wales I spent four years in the Netherlands. Here, the whole feel of things – the *cynefin* – is different. Instead of mountains, a molehill is an event in the flatlands. The land is partly claimed from the sea, and in that sense man-made. It has been fought over, colonized, occupied – not in that way so different from Wales. But the culture is profoundly different, influenced by commerce and materialism, and with a residual Calvinism that can be seen in paintings of faces, families, houses and households, as well as landscapes. The pressure of the human is everywhere.

For me, the common experience between living in Wales and living in the Netherlands was that it was determined by love.

This book contains several tributes to Welsh poets. In Wales, the tradition of praise poetry is ancient. One of its principal effects is to create visions of place. This came home to me vividly when I visited Laugharne and looked out on the estuary of the river Taf. At that moment I realized that what I was seeing was a scene Dylan Thomas had magicked into being. Waldo Williams did the same for his native Preseli. A visitor too may contribute, as David Jones did during his stay at Capel-y-ffin. The fact that Wales is a much-loved country is due in no small measure to its poets, whether writing in Welsh or English. The words *bro* and *cynefin* testify to this story.

www.ingramcontent.com/pod-product-compliance
Ingram Content Group UK Ltd.
Pitfield, Milton Keynes, MK11 3LW, UK
UKHW021911110325
456097UK00001B/67

* 9 7 8 1 8 4 8 6 1 9 7 0 8 *